SADNESS
IN THE
COLOR
YELLOW

To my loving grandpa

Larry G. Harris

It's hard to think about this being a fleeting feeling.
I've heard it all.
I know that sadness is necessary, and I know that there is no happiness without it.
My only question is, why?
Why must I experience this feeling of hopelessness before I can experience anything else?

I'm trying to understand how sadness and happiness
can coexist inside of me.

Contents

Sadness

In all its forms

This can't be the right date.

And this watch must be broken.

Months have gone by without me realizing.

Why is everyone moving on without me?

Don't they know I've suffered a great loss?

Don't they know I'm in pain and need more time?

Why is everyone moving on like the world didn't just end?

I had a friend who was yellow.
Everything about him was.
He was a good listener, generous,
and he was gentle.
His yellow started to change after a few months of
me knowing him.
Soon I saw his sadness take over and what once
was yellow,
was now blue.
We went our separate ways before I could see if
his color came back.

I hope his sadness found its way to the color
yellow and stayed just yellow.

I made the life I have now out of sticks and leaves.
It's unstable but it's been like this for years
and I'm afraid to start over.

Erase my memory

Sometimes I think it would've been better
to not know you at all than to know you
and experience the grief of losing you.

When sadness calls me, I want to be afraid.
I want to be so healed and happy that I run away
from it.
I want to have nothing in common with sadness
anymore.

What women my age know about friendship, they learned as a girl.
But me? I know nothing about what it means to be a good girlfriend.
I don't know what it feels like to be in one of those deep intense friendships
that I hear about.
I am just now learning about female friendship when my friends have known and experienced it all their lives.

I've tried but I can't seem to destroy
the image of me that everyone has in their head.
I think it's easier for them to hold onto the
weak and sad version of me.
That version was easy to run over
and manipulate.

I'm starting to see that without that version, I am
of no use to them.

Let me grow

I feel confined to these walls.
Never truly experiencing life and all it has to offer.
Never leaving and never growing.
Let me go.

I don't want to be an angry person anymore.
It's exhausting and not fair to my mind and body.
Why can't I break this cycle?
How will I ever be happy if I'm always
surrounded by
negative people with negative words?
I am a product of my environment.

My father filled his plate with expectations and
when
it became too full, he got up and walked away.
I was a child.
I didn't know what was expected.
I would have accepted you with whatever you
had.

Heartbreak looks like crying for hours, falling asleep,
and waking up with sore eyes and a sore throat.
It's going to the store and going straight to the snack aisle
to buy all the junk food you can find.
It's eating a pint of ice cream
while watching rom-coms.

Heartbreak looks like balling myself up
and hiding under the covers, not being able to leave my room for days.
Heartbreak looks like continuing to love you
while starting to hate myself.

If I were a flower, it would be an honor to be
picked by someone.
I wouldn't be upset that a stranger took me from
my home.
It would show me that I'm worthy
and beautiful.
So beautiful they couldn't resist
the urge to pick me, take me home, put me in a
nice vase,
and place me somewhere everyone could see.

Is this house my home?

The dinner table stays set but never touched.
The living room is only used for holidays or
"family bonding" times.
The kitchen is used but one at a time.
The house creaks and screams all over.
What kind of "home" is this?
I don't belong here, and I don't have space here.
I'm outgrowing this place, but I keep cutting parts
of myself to fit.
I'm trying to fit somewhere I clearly don't, and the
sad part is,
I'll keep doing it.
I'll keep cutting parts of myself to fit because I
want this house to
so badly be a home.

6:09pm

This moment right here feels so familiar.
The atmosphere, the breeze, the smell,
and this feeling.
It's so familiar.
The light from outside brightening up my room,
and me sitting here thinking.
I've been here once before.

July came and went and so did August.
By September I had forgotten about what
happened
but by October, I found myself breaking down
in the kitchen while making breakfast.
By January I had forgotten again and had to be
reminded that
you weren't here anymore.

I go through the first four stages of grief
repeatedly.
Never making it to acceptance.

I want someone to experience and write about me.
I want to for once, be someone's muse.

When I had a nightmare and came to you
for comfort, I wanted you to tell me that it was
going to be okay, maybe check under the bed and
in the closet.
Not brush it off and yell at me.
That night, I slept with tears in my eyes and with
the blankets over my head.

I miss the smell and color of childhood.
It was much brighter, and it always smelled like candy.
I miss the big dreams and goals I had for myself.
Everything seems so small and out of reach now.

I don't recognize the person I've become.
It feels like I went to bed one night and woke up an adult.
In place of watching cartoons all day, playing with my barbies, and running around with my friends,
I now go to work and I'm lucky if I can watch an episode of my favorite show,
I go to school for five hours every day,
and I now have bills to pay.
I'm not a kid anymore and I'll never be a kid again.

A goodbye letter

I know your heart will never beat for me the same
but please give me this one thing.
Let me love you until my love runs out.
Let me continue to feel.
Let me love you, hate you, grieve you,
and then accept the outcome.
Then and only then will I leave.

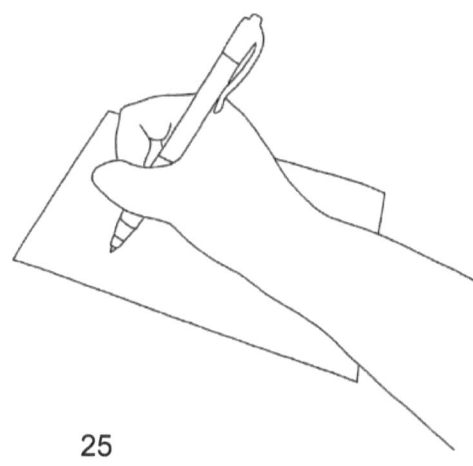

A couple of weeks before my senior graduation,
family and friends lined up to ask me the scary
question
that's been asked every year since freshman year.
"What do you want to be?"
I didn't answer because I wasn't sure, but I knew
they
would ask again next year and I knew that by
then, I'd know.

Although I still didn't know what I wanted to be,
when the next year came,
I was waiting for the question.
I had been thinking and I wanted to share
what I thought.
I wanted to share that it had been a struggle and I
still wasn't sure.
I waited and waited and still, nothing.
I didn't know that the day I walked out of my
graduation dinner would be the
last day I would be asked
"What do you want to be when you grow up?"
and
"What are your plans for the future?"

I like to think I'm kind but
the truth is, I'm a horrible person.
I'm bad at forgiving people and
I hold anger and bitterness in my heart
for people who don't even remember my name.

Cake batter

I don't like eating and I don't like eating in the
cafeteria.
There are too many eyes and too many people
telling me
with their facial expressions that I should be
ashamed of myself.
I like going to the bathroom.
It's quiet and its easier for me to do what I need to
do.
All the girls do it.
It's a normal thing.
"This, this will make me beautiful."
I say to myself as I kneel, take my finger, and put
my head over the toilet.

I don't want your love.
It comes from a place of terror.
Your love puts holes in the wall
and bruises on my body.

My child is my younger self

She's missing and I can't find her.
I ignored her for so long, she got up and walked
away.
I checked near the rocks I used to collect, On the
slide and swing set
at the park, In the toy aisle at the store,
and in front of the dinosaur exhibit at the science
center but nothing.
I know that if I don't find her soon, I'll lose her
forever.

Sometimes I think about buying a plane ticket
to the nearest state with a beach and just sitting
out there to write.
I'd write about my feelings while smelling the
fresh air and watching the waves crash
against each other.
Hearing the laughter of kids as they run around
and
seeing couples walk the beach while holding
hands
is something so peaceful and beautiful.

He told me to explain the type of love I want, and I said:

The type that excitement feels like.

The type that makes me tingly all over.

The type that feels like I'm on a roller coaster and it's going down fast.

This is the type of love I want to experience and feel.

Things left unsaid are good.

They keep us together and our emotions safe.

They keep doors from slamming shut and voices from being raised.

They keep us from having to heal from the things that might've been said.

Things left unsaid hold things together with cheap glue and with every truth and conversation, things start to fall apart.

I used to think people were crazy for wanting to
keep old things
from loved ones that had passed away.
I used to think it was weird for them to run
around searching for
memories of them in letters, pictures, and
messages.
Now that I've experienced loss, I get it.
I get the emptiness you feel and the want to just
be with them again and in the presence of their
things.

The people closest to me have a bad habit of
inviting unwelcome guests back into my life.
They fill my head with bible scriptures about
forgiveness and kindness.
Before I know it, I'm back on speaking terms with
them
and I'm sharing all my secrets.

I am uncertain about myself.

I think a lot but not about the things that matter.

I cry a lot but over the smallest things that aren't significant.

And I apologize a lot.

Mostly for things that aren't in my control.

I think something is wrong with me.
I don't feel the same way other women
my age feel about children.
I don't feel like a piece of me is missing and
only a baby will make me whole.
I don't feel like all the bad things about me will go
away
once I become a mother.
Being a mother is not something that I want and
because of that,
I think something is wrong with me.

Lets laugh, cry, and enjoy each other today
for tomorrow is a new day and you will cease to
exist to me.
We will go our separate ways and pretend like
nothing happened between us.
We will hang out with different people and soon
get jobs in different states.
We will start families and soon, we will be a
funny story we tell our family and friends.

Is it wrong to say that I think writing my first
suicide note
was the start of my future story telling career?
Expressing my feelings in that note released
something inside of me
that made me want to keep writing.
Writing is my escape.
When I write, I can express myself and
be vulnerable in ways I could never be in person.

A life of my own

Not a life for my mom.
Not a life for my dad.
A life of my own.
Away from this pattern of life
that was set up for me.
I want a life with meaning and
one worth living.
I don't want to live for others.
I want a life where my purpose is made
clear to me.
Maybe then, I wouldn't be so reliant and
consumed with what others have to say
about me and my life.

How selfless of you to take my burdens and
fears and carry them with you and how selfish
of me to let you do that.
I want to love like you.
You love me so much that you offer to take my
baggage
and carry it as yours.
You love me so much that you continue to do this.
You've given me everything and
more and I don't deserve you.

Half of me

I want you to know that it's okay to reach out to
me.
I want you to.
I want you to be comfortable talking to me again.
I miss you and I hope that you know that.
I hope you feel it.
I love you and I'm going to keep loving you until
I take my last breath, but even then, I won't stop.
I want you to think about me the way I think
about you.
To miss me the way I miss you.
And to love me, the way I love you.

Every time I start to remember, pieces of the house
I built for myself start to crumble.
Tears start to stain my shirt and leave my eyes red
and puffy.
Every time I remember, the people that I forgave
start
to look like enemies again.
When I remember, I cancel plans because I know
the thoughts will
leave me paralyzed for the day.

I'm mature for my age.
At least that's what he said.
With the promise of friendship, I was willing
to do anything he told me to do.
With stories of how everyone was doing it and
how it was normal, I believed him.
It felt weird and I knew it wasn't right but he
saw me for what I could be and
because of that, I stayed.

When you're a kid, you'll do almost anything to
be accepted.
I wanted to be accepted.

I want to be a human with needs and
desires but how do I achieve this and still
have people in my life?
How do I please others while also trying
to please myself?
This has never been done and
I'm not sure it ever will be done.

Pulling at the stitches

I cover them up.
I hate the way they look and
I hate what they represent.
I hate that whenever something similar to
my trauma happens, a scar bleeds.
I hate that whenever I try to let someone in,
A scar from a previous situation starts to ache,
reminding me that I shouldn't.

I believe in wishing on fallen eyelashes
and that shooting stars come right when
you need them.
I believe in soulmates and
that good things come to those who wait.
I believe people can truly change.

My strength.
You make me feel like I can do anything
I set my mind to.
You're my shoulder when I need one.
You help me see the beauty in myself and in
others.
My weakness.
This is sometimes stronger than my strength.
You have the ability to tear me down.
Whenever you feel like it, you take your shoulder
and walk away, leaving me alone and with
nothing
but a broken neck.

If love brings out the best in people,
but will eventually bring out the worst in them,
how can it be this great thing that everyone is in
search of?
If love at some point will hurt you whether it's
heartbreak or death,
why does everyone want to experience it?
Just by searching we break our own hearts.
Do we love because we like to suffer?

Me and my box

In the beginning, the box I had was the right size, maybe even a little too big.

I picked it out a while ago and didn't plan on picking out a different one.

My plan was simple.

I was ready to go so I needed to start packing.

It's not like it would take a long time.

At the time, my whole life could fit into half of the box I had.

I saw no point in going out and trying to find things to fill it up with.

I was content with everything that was inside.

I was okay with how I was living and how short notice me leaving would be.

I always thought about how funny and sad it was that my whole life could fit into one medium sized box.

That was my mindset a while ago.

Since then, I've changed routes.
I've been searching for a life without the feeling of
hopelessness and depression.
And I think I've found it.
The box that I had at the beginning is too small for
me now.
The love and memories that I have collected are
too big to fit inside of it.
Down this road of self-discovery, I have found the
will to live,
and I am not ready to stop here.
I want to live.
I want to keep going.
I want to keep searching for things that bring me
joy and that fill up my box.
I lost myself in the beginning but now I am ready
to find her and get her back.

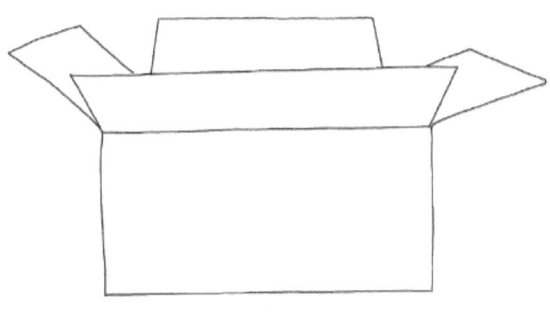

Let my empty room and my
empty presence haunt you.
Let the silence remind you of what you lost.
Let the pictures around the house remind
you of the girl you broke.

When things were bad, I would take away
the things that I loved the most as a way
of punishing myself.
Without the things that made me, me,
I became a boring person with nothing
to offer others or myself.
This was probably the biggest mistake I ever
made.

I'm good at making a six-player game work for one.
I'm good at blinding in with the things around me like a chameleon.
I'm good at observing and mimicking the things that others do.
I'm good at pretending because when I pretend for too long,
I start to lose myself.

You watch them from afar.

You pray and wish nothing but the best for them.

You watch them move on with their life while you slowly do the same.

These are the things you do when you love someone
who doesn't love you back.

In another universe we aren't strangers, and we aren't enemies.

In another universe we actually enjoy each other's company.

We talk about life together and we share our hobbies with each other.

We set aside two days out of the week and we catch up on each other's lives.

In another universe I have nothing and I am nothing without my sibling but

in this one, I am everything and more without mine.

Three.

That's how many parenting books I found on the bookshelf.

Three.

I see now that I was the one treating you like a burden.

My lack of communication made things hard.

It made you question your worth and your ability as a mother.

I'm sorry.

You were a 21-year-old girl trying to make sure everything was perfect

for her child and I made that hard for you.

Mother, do you grieve for the person you could have been without children?

Do you regret how your life turned out?

Would you do things differently if you had the chance?

A friend or foe?

How many times are we going to do this
depression?
How many times are you going to break my heart
by keeping me here?
The life that I must live unwillingly is one of the
greatest losses I have encountered.

It's been two weeks since we last talked.

This will be good for us, right?

Starting over and meeting new people?

Sometimes I want to call and check in, but I know I shouldn't.

I don't like that I have to think twice before sending you a funny post.

I miss you but I know that if I allow you to come back, you'll bring all your old ways back.

Things will be miserable for us, so I won't reach out.

I'll write.

I'm a writer so it's what I do best.

I'll write for hours about you.

I'll write pages about you.

I'll continue to think about you, but I won't text or call.

I've never seen gentle love.
The type of love that is patient and
that doesn't give you the silent treatment when
upset.
The type of love that doesn't slam and lock doors.
I've never seen the type of love that doesn't take
your
voice away and leave you with a headache.

How can I convince you to stay?
I can see that you're starting to get bored and the
things that used to work,
don't work anymore.
We've been arguing for weeks and I know that if I
don't fix it now,
I'll lose you for good.

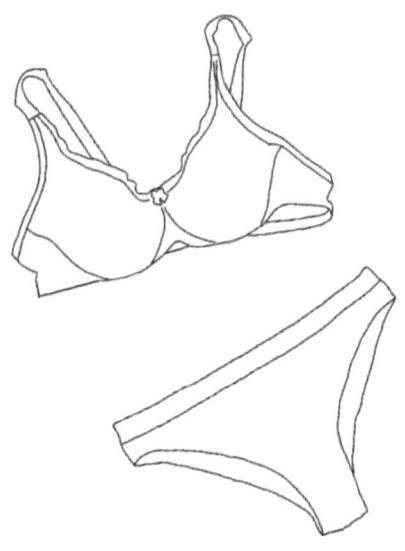

When flowers are blooming and
our favorite song is playing, everything is okay.

When flowers start to die and our song no longer
feels like our song, we start to get distant.
We only seem to like each other when the weather
is nice and
when everything is going good in our personal
lives.
We are no use to each other when we are both
sad.

I want to be a lovable person.

I want people to come around me because they know I'll make their day better.

I want people to feel safe around me.

I want to leave an impact on people.

I want them to think about my well-being and feelings and not think about if it's safe to talk to me or not.

I spent my whole childhood feeling like
a third option to everyone.
Feeling like a burden and feeling like
I was switched in the hospital.
Unrequited love from family was so confusing for
me.

The other women

On Monday, you showered me
with love and affection.
Holding my hand in public and sharing food with
me.
On Wednesday, you let my hand go while
we were walking and you looked disgusted
by me laughing at our inside joke.

I rip a piece of myself off every time
someone leaves so please stay.
I know that once you leave, I'll stop eating for
days.
I'll start to overthink everything between us.
I'll be stuck in bed unable to move for days.
So please stay.
If you love me, you'll stay.

When I see my friends, I find myself envying them
more than I miss them.
They have stories, they have life experiences,
they've moved away
and they've grown.
They live in apartments with their friends and go
out every weekend.
I still live at home and the most exciting thing I do
on weekends is binge watch my favorite TV show.

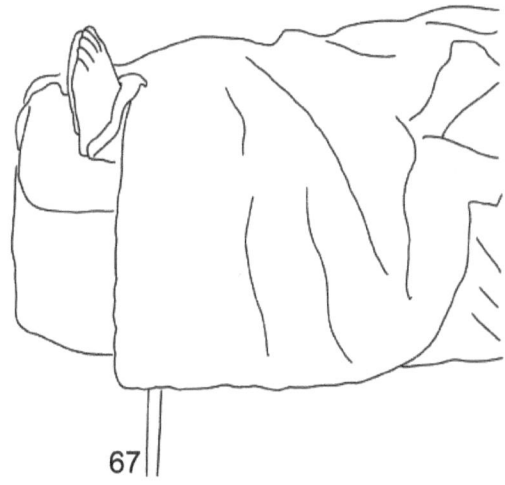

Loneliness follows me and when I hide,
it finds me every time.
The feeling sometimes passes through but
when life is hard, it stays a little longer to
remind me that it's all I have.

How do we come back after the horrible things
we did and said to each other?
Do we let time pass and act like nothing ever
happened?
Do we stay together and sit in silence like nothing
was ever said?
Why do we do this to each other and how do we
stop?

For the first time in my life, I didn't feel like an outsider in my family.

We were all going through the same thing.

For once, we all had something in common and something to talk about.

How silly of me to think that.

I looked back and realized that my pain was nothing compared to theirs.

Yes, I lost my grandpa, but my grandma lost her husband,

my mom and her siblings lost their dad,

and my grandpa's siblings lost their brother.

My anger is messy.
I lose my temper and I say and do hurtful things.
I yell and throw things.
I'm not a mean person.
I don't understand why I lash out and act this
way.

Once I realize what I've done, I spend the
morning patching holes
and apologizing to everyone.

Rest here.

I'll keep you inside of my pocket so whenever
I'm feeling weary, I can look down and know that
you are there and then remember that
you've always been there for me when needed.

Flowers around me started dying, the sky seemed to

always be grey, and I couldn't hear or understand laughter around me.

Eating started to feel like a job, and when I looked in the mirror, my face had changed.

My eyes were lower, and my eyebags were darker.

My body was always sore, my hair started falling out, and it seemed to rain a lot, in fact, it seemed to never stop raining.

I should've seen the signs sooner.

These things started when I met you and stayed when you left.

To my younger self

There was another setback.
I know I've been making a lot of excuses and I'm sorry.
I'm sorry I can't heal you properly and give you what you want and need.
I've been trying for a while and still, nothing.
Would you be upset with me if I decided to give up?

74

We had time.

I should've stayed and let you love me.

I regret not showing you more of me.

I feel like if I did, you would've stayed.

You would've loved the parts of me that I hid so well and

I know now that you would've accepted them.

When your friends can't make it, when you need
to vent,
and until someone or something better comes
along,
I am here.
You put me on your shelf and pick me up
whenever
you need me.
I am the placeholder friend.

I don't want to be strong anymore.

I want to fall apart and be held in someone's arms.

My shoulder is wet from all the tears, and it hurts from

always having to be the one to hold others' head up.

I want a shoulder to cry on.

I want to fall apart because I've been strong

for a long time and it hurts pretending.

When you wake

One day you're going to wake up and
come to your senses about our relationship.
You're going to realize that I've done nothing but
hold you back from others and opportunities.
You'll get ready to leave and see that your bags
are already packed and by the door.
You'll realize that you never unpacked them, and
they have been sitting there for months.
You'll get your things and walk out the door and I
won't stop you because
I know what you deserve and it's not me.

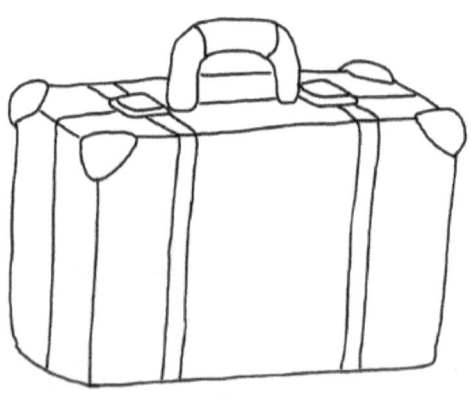

The monsters that torment me aren't hiding in my closet or under my bed.
They live inside of me, sit at the dinner table for meals, and sleep under the same roof as me.
Some of them call me family and some call me friend.

My sadness is just sadness right now but
I'm praying that it will soon be in the color
yellow.

The Color Yellow

When it comes to happiness, I want her to welcome
me with open arms and a smile on her face every
morning.
I want her to meet me in the hallway and follow
me out the door.

I am here to create and to love.
To water myself and the ones I love daily.
If the meaning of life is what I make it,
I plan to make it beautiful.

If I could go back and tell my younger self
something,
it would be to stop worrying.
So now I'm telling you.
You're doing fine.
You're not a failure because you don't have what
others your age have.
You're doing fine and there is no need to stress.
These are your young adult years.
I don't think you should spend them trying to
chase this and that.
I think you should slow down and just *be*.

I'm exhausted.

It's so exhausting hating myself.

Hating my body, my voice, my hair, and my face.

I'm tired.

I'm ready to love myself.

I'm ready to work towards self-love.

Living in a toxic house while
trying to heal and grow is like your house being
on fire and
you trying to use a cup of water to put it out.
It's not going to work.
You can't continue on with your healing journey while
everything around you is on fire.
Until those flames are completely put out or until
you work up
the courage to leave the house, nothing is going to change.
Your house will eventually burn with you inside
if you don't get up and walk away.

I had a dream that I passed every opportunity that
came my way.
In this dream, I didn't even acknowledge them.
Overtime I started to grow resentment towards
the missed opportunities
and those who took them.
When I woke up, I realized that it wasn't a dream.
It was my reality.
I'm always in a rush.
I don't like starting things when there could be
something better out there.
Because of this, I'm always left with nothing.
I wish I would've known sooner that I had time.

You think you didn't do much and wasted your
day
but I think you did so much.
You kept yourself alive and
I applaud you for that.

The people that you invite into your life are very important.

Like-Minded people who love and care about you will help you grow.

Destructive people care about nothing, not even themselves.

They will bring you down with them if you let them.

And when it comes to the past and the memories it holds,
let's learn to let go of its hand.
Let the past be a distant cousin that only comes to visit on
holidays or birthdays but never both and that doesn't stay for too long.

Growth is not a one-time thing.

You can't just read self-help books for a month,

decide you're better,

and move on with your life.

You should constantly be growing.

Trauma doesn't always make a person stronger.
If your trauma made your skin thin, that's
understandable.
What you went through was hard.
I want you to know that I'm rooting for you
every single day.

You deserve a gentle kind of love.
The kind of love that talks things out and tells you why
they're upset instead of ignoring you.
You deserve a patient and full kind of love.

About three months after my grandpa passed
away,
my sadness started to turn into the color yellow.
Good things started to happen to me, but grief
kept me from enjoying them.
At one point I even started to tell myself that it
had been long enough and
that it was time to move forward.

Don't make the same mistake I did by thinking
you're okay sooner than you are.
Take the time to heal.
Don't push yourself back into the world when
you're not ready.

Forgive yourself for past mistakes.
Accept the things you cannot change and
don't get stuck trying to understand
where it all went wrong.

Things are going to be different starting with me.
I don't want to be so consumed with a man that I
lose myself.
I don't want to be so consumed with work that I
lose my kids,
and I don't want to be so consumed with what
others have to say,
that I lose myself.

Knowing that this isn't all I'll ever be
makes me hopeful for tomorrow.
I'll try again tomorrow.

I can't seem to stop for long enough to accept
the love I'm being given.
I love and I want to receive and feel the love that
others are giving me
but I seem to just be collecting it and not really
feeling it.

I still stop by the toy aisle in every store I go to.
I pick flowers, collect rocks that look like they might
have crystals inside, and I still suck my fingers when
I'm tired or stressed.
I like going to the park, and I still ride my bike around my neighborhood
listening to music.
Yes, I do these things because I enjoy them but the little girl inside of me
enjoys them more.
I continue to do these things for her.
They make her happy and they make her feel seen.

You are eighteen years old.

You've seen other teenagers already moved out and

in their first apartment, now you're pushing yourself and working

more hours than you should.

Wow.

Social media does a good job making us feel bad about where we are in life.

There is no set date or time on when you should have life figured out.

Take your time with everything that you do.

When the time is right and you're ready,
what you were waiting for would have been
waiting for you
and will be right there to greet you with open
arms.

I keep photos and little notes from people I don't talk to anymore.
I keep them in a little box underneath my bed.
I keep the box not because I think the friendship will be rekindled but
because it's nice to have proof of the love I received and shared.

The worst thing you can do to someone you love
is love them too much.
Your love shouldn't be smothering.
Your love shouldn't hinder their goals.

The day you walk away from that toxic situation
is not
the day things get better.
Things might even get harder once you leave.
It's going to take time.
The commitment to yourself needs to be stronger
than
your desire to return to that situation.

Where is your community?
Who is there to help you when it feels like sadness
loves you more?
When the sun sets and your thoughts take over,
who is there for you?

You packed your grief up in a bag.

It's yours so you want it close to you.

You carry it everywhere but now it's getting too heavy.

You want to put it down but it's yours.

You want to talk to someone about it

but it's yours and they probably wouldn't understand.

You put the bag down and you open it up.

It's yours.

You're the only one who can deal with it.

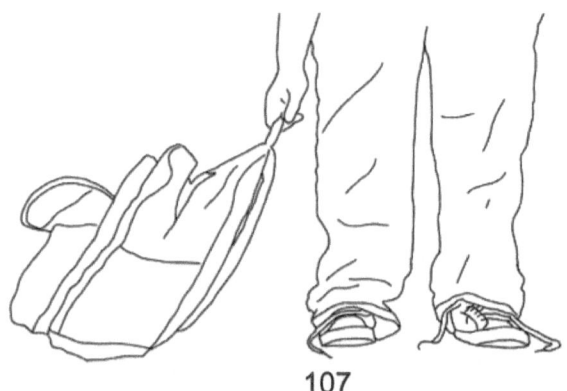

I can't forgive you, but I can.
I care about myself and the people in my life so,
I will forgive you.
I will forgive you because if I don't,
I'll end up losing myself in anger and in hatred
and losing the people I care about in disgust
and in sadness.
I thought I could not forgive you
but I can and I will.

Just being you is enough.

That empathy of yours makes you, you.
To be understanding and sensitive towards others
is a gift in a world filled with hate.

That laugh that you hate so much makes you,
you.
It puts a smile on others face when they need it.

I'm going to decorate my home the way I want and

paint each room a different color.

I'm going to hang out with people that make me feel good and

I'm always full after dinner so I'm going to eat dessert before my meals.

I'm going to wear what I want no matter the fabric or design and

I'm going to eat when I'm hungry.

Not worrying about the day, time, or size of the plate.

Loving you from the other side was easier.

It kept friends around and rumors away.

It makes me sick knowing that at some point in time,

what others thought of me was more important than

what you thought of me.

Why did I treat you like that God?

I'm so sorry.

You go out of your way to not upset people.
You dull your light, and you don't speak up for yourself.
You hold the emotions of others, and you accept the
bare minimum from everyone you meet.
Why do you do that?

There are many things to love.
The feelings that your childhood friends give you
when you
guys hang out for the first time after a while,
the rain and leaves falling in October, your
favorite song
on a bad day, and long walks in the park.

I'm sorry that someone told you your love wasn't real or
enough because you decided to leave and not continue
fighting for the relationship.
Sometimes we walk away *because* we love them.

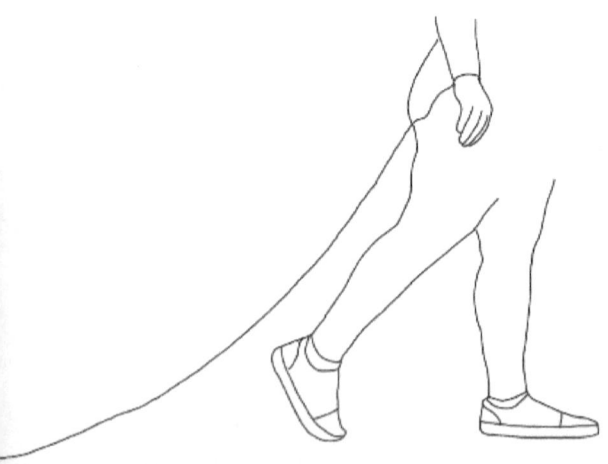

Versions of you come and go like the seasons and I think that's a good thing.

We should always be growing and changing.

Be happy that you will soon change and be in a new place in life.

You'll look back and miss your old self but not enough to go back.

I want to know your favorite color and animal but
first
tell me about the things you're passionate about.
Tell me all your dreams.
The big and small ones.
Tell me about your family and about the guy
you've been
best friends with since elementary school.
Tell me about how you would like to be
remembered.
Are you living life to the fullest or are you here
just surviving?
As we end the night and are walking around, tell
me your favorite color
and the kind of music you like.

Tell me about the last book you read as we
walk the five minutes to the ice cream shop.

Her color

I love the way:

Her hair falls in front of her face when she's
focused on writing,
black and curly.
She sits in the grass while painting or reading,
green with little yellow flowers all around.
Her skin shines in the sun, brown with a honey
color.
Her brown lips part as she's about to smile with
those
beautiful white teeth, amazing.

I'm sorry but I have no room for other people's
sadness anymore.
Usually, I can take it because if I can't, who am I?
If I am no longer of use to people, who am I?
I used to be good at carrying baggage that wasn't
mine but now...
now things are different.
My baggage is heavier than it's ever been
so, there's no room for anyone else's.

You deserve the good things you think about and want but are too afraid to ask and pray for. You are good enough and deserving.

And I know there are some things I need to work on.

I can be a little quieter in the mornings and I can speak more when I see people I know in the hallway.

I can text or call first at least once, and if I'm already washing dishes,

I can wash them all.

I can listen more and argue less, and I can speak up more about

the things that bother me.

I want to talk to you over dinner.
While we're eating, our song will play and
we'll laugh thinking about the first time we heard
it.
I'll tell you I love your laugh and you'll tell me to
shut up but I won't.
I tell you I love you all the time, but this time is
different because tonight
I tell you I'm *in* love with you.

How many times are you going to leave yourself
without
to chase after others?
How many times are you going to let yourself
down while uplifting others?
You have left yourself stranded one too many
times and
it's time to stop.

If I grow up and change my ways now, a house somewhere in Colorado
will sit calling me.
Waiting for me to make it a home.
I can't wait to one day cover the walls with pictures of the family
I created for myself and to have the people I love most fill the rooms
with laughter and love.

I know life is hard right now and giving up seems like
the best thing to do but do you want to know something
cool about being young?
We have time to figure things out.
If you don't like where you are right now, you can change that.
And if you don't like the new version you created, you can change again.

Life isn't all clouds and rain.
You realized this the morning after the breakup.
You started breathing again and the clouds
over your head went away.

You say you're over the situation, but you space out
for hours thinking about it.
You say you're over him, but you think about him
when your current partner does something that's
familiar to you.
When the day is good, you reminisce and miss the
good and bad times.
The lingering memories of the past will be your
downfall.

Self to self

Maybe after your heart breaks and
your days are sad, you can come back to me?
I'll try my best to help you through it.
You don't always have to stop loving me
when they stop loving you.

If you can see the light at the end of the tunnel and
you're working towards reaching that light, I would say your sadness
is in the color yellow.
A lot of people get lost or get too scared on their way out but
I want you to keep going.
Imagine how beautiful it's going to look once you're
out of that dark place.

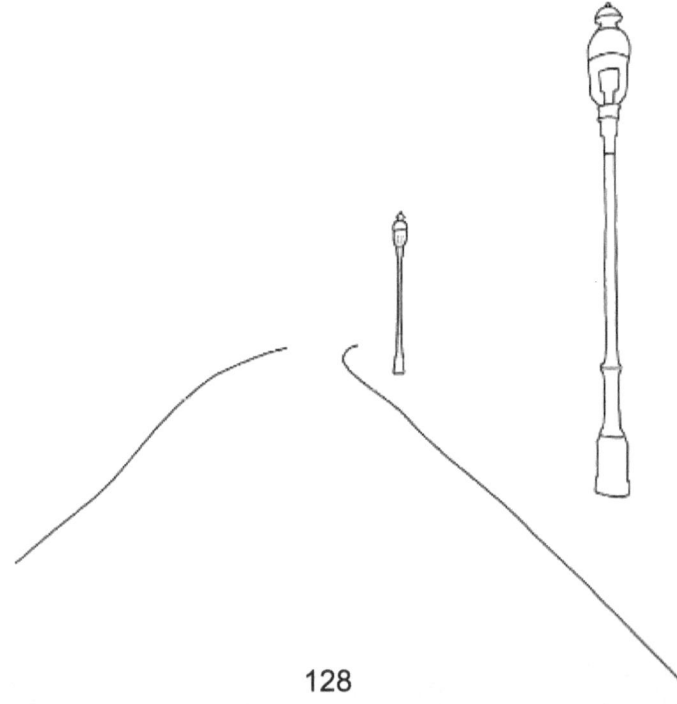

Stay away from those who make you feel like
your experiences are not valid.
Stop hanging out with people who like to
bring up what you went through and invalidate it.

Resentment grows where love does not.
I'm learning to let go of feelings of regret and
jealousy
and fill nothing but love in my pot.

Because we changed

We will wake up in the morning and eat breakfast
together
while we talk about the things we should do for
the day.
We will go and make the bed so it's harder to get
back in it later.
We will go grocery shopping together and
recommend things
that we think the other might like.
After, we'll go home and just be with each other.

You do something that upsets me but instead of
walking away,
I tell you and we talk about it.
Afterwards, we read and laugh and later watch
movies together.
All because we changed.

To love someone and let them go
does not make you weak.

Sadness becomes of the broken hearted and the way to fix that is to let yourself grieve. Grieve, practice self-care, and remember that healing takes time.

The smell of cookies on Christmas eve.

The sun peeking through my curtains
causing me to wake up.

Looking up at the stars on a warm night.

Watching my favorite romance movie for
the third time in a row.

Walking in the park with ice cream
on a hot summer day.

Blasting my favorite song while I
dance around in my room.

Watching the sun rise and set.

These things.

These are the things I live for.

Come home now.

I fear that if you stay away any longer,

you'll forget what things look like and where

things are.

I'll keep the grass cut and the plants watered for

you.

I want you to know that it's never too late to come

back home.

When life gives you a good friend,
you hold on to them for as long as you can.
You show up to celebrate wins with them and
you sit down to listen and help them through the
bad times.
When life gives you a good friend,
you encourage each other to continue going.

I still haven't found what I'm looking for.

I don't know what it is, but I know something is missing.

I'm going to keep searching.

When the timing is right, maybe the path of life will lead me there.

For me, my color yellow in the midst of my
sadness
was getting my first car, getting the job I applied
for,
my art getting recognized, meeting and enjoying
new people,
and getting opportunities handed to me left and
right.
I couldn't enjoy any of these things because how
could I?
How could I enjoy these things in the middle of
grieving?
My sadness is in the color yellow and that should
be a good thing but
I don't know how to handle it.

Cover art and illustrations by:
Deunvion Smith

Other books by Deunvion Smith:
Because you exist, I write
Watering dead flowers

www.ingramcontent.com/pod-product-compliance
Lightning Source LLC
Chambersburg PA
CBHW052146170626
46812CB00004B/1612